June O'Sullivan
and Nausheen Khan

fantastic ideas to
encourage diversity and inclusion

HOW DO YOU FEEL TODAY?

FEATHERSTONE

FEATHERSTONE
Bloomsbury Publishing Plc
50 Bedford Square, London, WC1B 3DP, UK
29 Earlsfort Terrace, Dublin 2, Ireland

ISBN: PB: 978-1-4729-9389-2; ePDF: 978-1-4729-9390-8

2 4 6 8 10 9 7 5 3 1

Series design by Lynda Murray

Printed and bound in India by Replika Press Pvt. Ltd.

To find out more about our authors and books visit www.bloomsbury.com and sign up for our newsletters

Contents

Introduction 4

Difference and diversity

Diwali 6

How do you feel? 8

Love the way we are.................................... 9

Painting my feelings 10

Magic carpet 12

Art exhibition 13

Let's learn Makaton................................... 14

Father's and Mother's Day cards................ 15

Drag queen story time............................... 16

Toy museum 17

The pomegranate cake 18

The colour of me 20

Penguins of the world................................ 21

Celebrating warmth and empathy 22

Learning about our families........................ 23

I can be anything....................................... 24

Diversity, friendship and kindness.............. 25

Exploring our feelings................................ 26

Fingerprints 27

Baby you're fantastic!................................ 28

What's in the box?..................................... 29

Time machine 30

Pen pals.. 31

Careers fair 32

I baked a cake for Christmas 34

My space... 36

Communication generation 37

Respect, kindness and empathy

The friendship quilt................................... 38

The card factory 40

Let's play with my favourite toy.................. 41

The book hospital....................................... 42

Sofa talk 44

Thank you cards 45

The message tree....................................... 46

Empathy day 48

The zoo in our garden 49

World café 50

Parachute fun 52

Football... 53

Jigsaw 54

Helicopter 55

Fire lighting... 56

Games from different cultures.................... 57

In the community

Parent buddy scheme 58

Dorothy's tea party.................................... 59

Finding my place in the neighbourhood..... 60

Food bank 61

Encouraging staff to listen and think

Web of connectivity.................................... 62

Take my hand 63

Build a social inclusion network 64

Introduction

The best place to begin building inclusion is in the Early Years. This is the time when we can have the greatest impact in improving the life chances of our children. It's a time when they are open to learning and are influenced by the adults and experiences around them. As Early Years teacher practitioners we can create an inclusive experience for our children through understanding the structural barriers that sustain prejudice, injustice and inequality and by building greater social inclusion and engagement.

Many people working in the Early Years will say that being inclusive is central to their practice because they have been trained within a dominant philosophy that celebrates the uniqueness of each child balanced by a commitment to protect and nurture all children during their childhood. However, when you dig a little deeper, the concept of inclusivity and how it enables diversity is often misunderstood. Celebrating diversity and promoting inclusion should form part of our daily interactions with children and should permeate all of the experiences that we share with them. Tokenistic actions, however well meaning, are not enough; diversity and inclusion must be integral to every aspect of our practice. This book is here to help you explore the concept of inclusivity through activities and conversations at your own pace and in a way that builds the knowledge and confidence necessary to lead and learn in an inclusive setting.

In the Early Years we want to create an inclusive education that removes barriers to learning and participation and that recognises and responds to the impact of the structural inequalities that come from poverty, racism, religious intolerance, ageism, gender and disability inequalities in our settings. By creating inclusion, we enable diversity to thrive.

Inclusion is ultimately about treating each other kindly and, as Early Years staff, responding warmly and positively to each child's developing needs and interests. It is not a series of specific activities that are called diverse; rather, it's about seeing how we can give space for everyone by accepting people and creating conditions which enable everyone to be included. Inclusion is about how we uplift each other with kindness and acceptance. By creating a respectful pedagogy, we can ensure that we deliver an inclusive education that will allow diversity to thrive whilst promoting positive relationships with all children, parents, carers and the community.

Understanding difference and how children respond to it is very important if we are to develop and implement inclusive practice. Children are social and cultural beings, actively learning to make sense of their world. They assimilate information from experiences in various contexts: television, images, their own immediate family, their wider community and society generally, and from you, as an Early Years teacher practitioner!

Derman-Sparks* (1992) suggested that children between the ages of two and five are forming their self-identities, building social interaction skills, noticing differences, and becoming curious about gender, race, ethnicity and disability. We have a role to play in supporting children's learning so that what they learn is open and inclusive and mitigates them misunderstanding, which could lead to prejudice. During this time children also develop a rudimentary understanding of the concept of justice, as well as attitudes of acceptance, cooperation and sensitivity towards others.

We therefore need to create an environment where children are able to like who they are without needing to feel superior to anyone else. We also need to teach them to negotiate and adapt to differences, and understand and emotionally accept the common humanity that all people share. Inclusive pedagogy requires all staff to be very knowledgeable about children's development and understand the best ways to teach because an inclusive education will benefit all children by teaching them to respect and value each other.

This book contains activities and ideas that celebrate diversity and promote inclusion as part of something that we do every day.

It is structured into four main sections:

- Difference and Diversity focuses on activities that celebrate our own and each other's uniqueness and differences.

- Respect, Kindness and Empathy provides activities that help support children to see situations from other perspectives.

- In the Community includes activities that take an interest in the communities in which we are working to ensure that we celebrate the diversity around us.

- Encouraging Staff to Listen and Think provides activities that explore the fact that to be truly inclusive as practitioners we must reflect honestly on our own attitudes and experiences.

Ultimately, by paying attention to our understanding of diversity, by showing kindness to each other and by acknowledging the importance of constantly talking, listening and thinking, together we can build a shared view that makes a positive difference to how we respond to our children, staff, parents, carers and the community.

How to use this book

The pages are all organised in the same way. Before you start any activity, read through everything on the page so that you are familiar with the whole activity and what you might need to plan in advance.

What you need lists the resources required for the activity. These are likely to be readily available in most settings or can be bought or made easily.

What to do tells you step-by-step what you need to do to complete the activity.

Top tips are helpful hints to make an activity work well and have been learned from experience!

The **Health & Safety** tips are often obvious, but safety cannot be overstressed. In many cases, there are no specific hazards involved in completing the activity, and your usual health and safety measure should be enough. In others, there are particular issues to be noted and addressed.

Taking it forward gives ideas for additional activities on the same theme, or for developing the activity further. These will be particularly useful for things that have gone especially well or where children show a real interest. In many cases they use the same resources, and in every case they have been designed to extend learning and broaden the children's experiences.

What's in it for the children? tells you briefly how the suggested activities contribute to learning.

*Derman-Sparks, Louise (1992). "Reaching Potentials Through Anti-bias, Multicultural Curriculum", Chapter 8 in "Reaching Potentials: Appropriate Curriculum and Assessment for Young Children", Volume 1, Bredekamp, Sue & Rosegrant, Teresa (eds). Washington DC: National Association for the Education of Young Children.

Diwali

Celebrating with music, diyas and Rangoli patterns

What you need:

- Access to the internet to research the story or share the book *Rama and Sita* by Malachy Doyle
- A device to play audio
- Indian music
- A range of diyas (lamps used during Diwali)
- Air-drying clay to make diyas
- Powder paints or coloured rice to make Rangoli patterns (colourful designs created on floors or tabletops)

What to do:

1. Research the story of Rama and Sita and how the festival of Diwali was created.
2. Tell the story to the children during circle time, exploring the victory of good over bad. Explain that Diwali is celebrated by Hindus, Sikhs and Jains all over India and around the world.
3. Explore how the word 'Diwali' comes for the Sanskrit word 'deepavali', meaning 'rows of lighted lamps'.
4. Show the children pictures of people celebrating Diwali and the diyas that you have gathered, while you play some music. Encourage the children to hold and feel the diyas, whilst emphasising the importance of light.
5. Invite the children to make their own diyas using the clay. An adult may need to help to make the clay soft.
6. Whilst the diyas are drying, support the children in creating their Rangoli patterns.
7. Once the diyas have dried, the children can paint them, place a tea light inside them and display them around their Rangoli patterns.

Top tip

Research Rangoli patterns and show children some examples of simple or complex designs as a way to explore mathematical concepts.

✚ Health & Safety

If children are using tea lights and matches, close adult supervision is required. If you make an Indian sweet, be aware of allergies and dietary requirements.

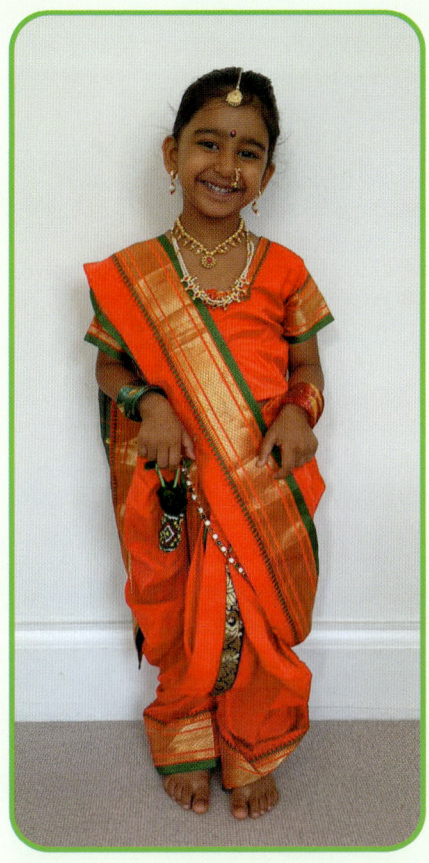

What's in it for the children?

Diwali is a popular marker in many people's calendars; learning about Diwali will help those children who don't celebrate this festival to appreciate other cultures and traditions. Children who celebrate Diwali will feel included and recognised in the setting. The diya activity can provide a chance for children to take part in some risky play by lighting a match to light their tea light (with close adult supervision).

Taking it forward

- Invite the children to dance to the Indian music.

- Make an Indian sweet for the children to take home.

How do you feel?

Using toys as props

What you need:

- A teddy, soft toy or puppet
- Photographs of people showing a range of emotions, such as sad, happy, angry and so on

Top tip

Keep the group small and it may lead to an activity that continues over several days.

What's in it for the children?

Children often have an affinity with a soft toy or a puppet and welcome such friends into their world. Using these toys as props will provoke conversations between the children and will help them to describe how they feel, which will provide the first steps towards building strategies to deal with emotions.

Taking it forward

- Create a storytelling activity – ask the children to devise a story about feelings, write out the story and then read it back to the children so that they can act it out.

Health & Safety

Be mindful that a child may disclose something needing further investigation. Practitioners need to have a good understanding of their setting's safeguarding procedures.

What to do:

1. Gather the children in a small group.
2. Ensure that the children are comfortable and free from distractions.
3. Introduce the activity to the children talking to them about words that describe feelings, such as happy, sad, upset, angry, scared, confused. Use the photographs to accompany each of the feelings so that the children can relate a physical expression to the spoken word.
4. Sit the teddy or toy on your lap and tell the children how the toy is feeling and why.
5. Ask the children what they think about this feeling. For example, why do they think the toy feels sad? Have they ever felt sad?
6. Ask the children what they could do to help the toy not to feel sad, angry or scared.

Love the way we are

Taking inspiration from *Elmer*

What you need:

- *Elmer* by David McKee
- An Elmer toy (optional)
- A large piece of cardboard with the outline of an elephant drawn onto it
- Paints, crayons or pens
- Paper
- Decorations, such as ribbons and jewels (optional)

Top tip

Encourage conversations focusing on the fact that although we all look different, inside we are the same.

What's in it for the children?

The children will learn that we are all different and that being different is not to be feared. In addition to this, the children will extend their social skills as they work together and develop their language skills through the introduction of new vocabulary.

Taking it forward

- Focus on the children's creativity skills and support them in designing their own Elmers.
- Carry out some research with the children to find out about different types of elephants and where they live in the world.

What to do:

1. Read the story *Elmer* to the children.
2. Use the toy as a prop or share the pictures from the book so the children can really see Elmer's colours.
3. Ask the children questions about the book, such as, 'Why didn't Elmer want to be different?', 'Why is it OK to be different to other people?', or 'Why do the other elephants look up to Elmer?'
4. Suggest that the children create their own Elmer based on their own skin colours.
5. Either draw shapes within the elephant for the children to colour, or hand out paper for the children to use, which can then be stuck onto the elephant.
6. Ask the children to colour their shape based on their own skin colour.
7. When the elephant has been coloured or the paper has been added to the elephant, ask the children to choose a name (the children could vote for their favourite).
8. Celebrate the beauty of each child's different colour on the new elephant and display the artwork for the children, parents and carers to see.

Painting my feelings

Exploring emotions through art

What you need:

- A book about emotions, such as *It's OK to Cry* by Molly Potter or *The Colour Monster* by Anna Llenas
- Paints (blue, red, purple, yellow, brown and grey)
- Paint brushes
- Paper
- Aprons
- Easels or space for the children to make paintings

What to do:

1. Sit the children comfortably in a small group.
2. Introduce the topic of feelings by talking about the language of emotions and feelings, such as happy, sad, angry, scared, tired and bored.
3. Ask the children what makes them feel these emotions whilst reinforcing the vocabulary.
4. Read the children a story about emotions.
5. Suggest to the children that they might like to paint how they feel using the following colours:
   - Sad = blue
   - Angry = red
   - Happy/joyful = yellow
   - Tired = brown
   - Scared/anxious = purple
   - Bored = grey

Top tip ⭐

There are some great books to help explore this topic, for example, Tom Percival's emotionally resonant *Big Bright Feelings* series.

➕ Health & Safety

Be mindful that a child may disclose something needing further investigation. Practitioners need to have a good understanding of the setting's safeguarding procedures.

What's in it for the children?

Children are in a safe and secure space to explore their emotions through colours, painting and speech.

Taking it forward

- Encourage the children to share their paintings with the group, talking about the emotions that they have painted.

- Introduce puppets so that the children can create a dramatic enactment of their paintings.

- Display the children's work or create an emotions display board for parents and carers.

- Work with the children to think of other emotions and choose colours to represent these feelings.

Magic carpet

Exploring the world

What you need:

- A small rug or carpet
- Access to the internet
- A world map or globe
- Photographs and artefacts from the chosen destination

Top tip ⭐

Is this the home country of any of the children in your setting? Perhaps Dorothy the Bear can visit? See page 59.

What's in it for the children?

The children can learn about the wider world and the people who live in it through a range of resources, including technology. The children will enjoy the magic carpet ride and will feel empowered to travel wherever they wish to go.

Taking it forward

- Teach the children even more about the people who live in their chosen destination, exploring their culture and traditions by including books, music and food.

What to do:

1. Organise a planning meeting with the children where they decide which country in the world they would like to visit. This can be somewhere they are familiar with, is relevant to them and their families, or that is completely new. When the children have chosen the country, gather some information and resources, such as a map, photos and artefacts from the chosen place.

2. To start the activity, invite the children to sit on the magic carpet and 'fly' to their chosen destination.

3. When they have 'landed' at their destination, using Google Earth, support the children to learn about the country by dropping the street view icon at the chosen location and having a look around.

4. Support the children's knowledge and understanding by using the resources that have been selected and talking to them about the place and the people who live there.

5. Encourage the children to compare where they live with the country they have chosen, looking for similarities and differences.

Art exhibition

Celebrating uniqueness and ability

What you need:

- Photos of famous paintings and sculptures from around the world
- A blank wall, section of a classroom or display board
- A range of open-ended resources including:
  - Paper
  - Paints
  - Natural materials
  - Recycled materials
  - Scissors
  - Air-drying clay
  - Sculpting tools

Top tip

Contact the local framing shop and ask for their off cuts to use for framing the children's artwork.

What to do:

1. Introduce the children to the concept of an art gallery, either by visiting a local gallery, or through sharing photos.
2. Prior to the activity, set up an art studio by:
   - Arranging the resources that are to be used according to colour and/or substance.
   - Displaying and labelling the tools that are to be used.
3. When planning the activity, allow a week of artwork so that the children have time to look at examples, try out ideas and practise until they are happy with their pieces.
4. During circle time, share with the children famous paintings and sculptures from around the world.
5. Help the children to decide what they will create as their showpieces. Share with them lots of examples of different types of art and let them choose, encouraging them to consider what they could create to represent themselves and their families.
6. Use the expertise within the setting by involving all members of staff who can show the children artworks and techniques from their own cultures.
7. When the children have decided what kind of artwork they would like to produce, support them in working with the various materials.
8. When the artwork has been created, it can be displayed and parents and carers invited in to view.

What's in it for the children?

This is a fun and celebratory activity that provides an opportunity for the children to learn more about art from around the world and from different cultures, as well as to celebrate and explore the different cultures within the setting. Perseverance and concentration will be developed through being creative, and the children will enjoy and feel a sense of pride in having their artwork displayed.

Taking it forward

- Contact a local art college or university and invite a student to come into the setting to support the project.

Let's learn Makaton

What the Jackdaw Saw

What you need:

- *What the Jackdaw Saw* by Julia Donaldson
- Advice from the Makaton charity: www.makaton.org

Top tip ⭐

Make time for a game of Makaton Charades during circle time.

What to do:

1. Read *What the Jackdaw Saw* to the children.
2. Ask the children what is happening in the story and how the animals communicate.
3. Teach the children the Makaton signs for 'happy', 'sad', 'scared' and 'cross'.
4. Ask the children how they think the Jackdaw felt when he could not understand what the animals were saying. Encourage the children to use the Makaton signs when giving their answers.
5. Ask the children how they think the Jackdaw felt when he could understand his friends by using the signs. Encourage the children to use the Makaton signs when giving their answers.

What's in it for the children?

The children will learn about the diverse and different ways we communicate and how we can use signs for this, especially when we cannot speak. This activity will also provide an opportunity for the children to show empathy and to understand how disability can affect people.

Taking it forward

- Send the activity home so families can learn the Makaton signs.
- Spend a session in 'silence' where children and adults have to communicate with each other without speaking.

Father's and Mother's Day cards

What makes a family?

What you need:

- A book about families, such as *And Tango Makes Three* by Peter Parnell and Justin Richardson or *My Family: Love and Care, Give and Share* by Lisa Bullard
- Card
- Envelopes
- Pens and paper
- A range of craft materials to decorate with

Top tip

Avoid the conveyor belt approach to making the cards. Take your time and do it in small groups over the week, so that the children can talk with one another and enjoy the conversations.

What's in it for the children?

This is a multi-layered opportunity that crosses all of the learning areas, such as helping children to work together, improving mark making and understanding writing for purpose. Most importantly, it provides an opportunity for the children to talk about their families in a small group and to understand that not all families look the same.

Taking it forward

- Make a family album featuring the children in the nursery using photos, pictures, drawings and quotes and put it in the book corner.

What to do:

1. Read a book about families to the children, for example *And Tango Makes Three* or *My Family*.
2. Discuss what makes a family, focusing on the fact that not all families have a mum and a dad – some have two mums or two dads, some have one mum or one dad. Some have step-dads or step-mums, some live with grandparents and so on.
3. Talk about the activity and who the children will design their cards for. If this is not a parent or carer, it can be anyone who is special to them, such as a grandparent, aunt or uncle.
4. Split the children into small groups and support them in making their cards.

Drag queen story time

Inspiring reading and acceptance of others

What you need:

- A drag queen wearing a suitable theatrical costume or a video of a drag queen reading a children's story. There are many available online.

Top tip

Communicate well; this activity may take some explaining to parents and carers who are unsure about inviting a performer into the setting.

What's in it for the children?

This activity provides an opportunity for staff to better understand that special events can combine children's learning with provoking wider adult debates. Ultimately, this benefits the children who always gain from more thoughtful and reflective staff. The activity is also lots of fun and the children will enjoy storytelling being brought to life.

Taking it forward

- Introduce the topic at a staff meeting to open up wider conversations about diversity.
- Initiate conversations among staff and parents about inclusivity and diversity.

What to do:

1. Write a letter to the parents and carers to inform them of the forthcoming event and to explain how the story time will take place. Clarify that the drag queen story time uses theatricality to provide a human alternative to viewing on screen. Provide an opportunity for parents and carers to ask any questions that they may have. It is unlikely that the children will have any issues with a dramatic person entering their space, but parents, carers and staff may have concerns.

2. Choose a drag queen who most fits your brief as performers have a wide range of characters and personas. Involve the children in this process.

3. Meet with the drag queen to discuss what books and props they will use, as well as to talk through any questions raised by staff, parents and carers.

4. Provide a list of the children's first names so that they can be fully included in the story time.

5. After the event, support the children in making and sending a thank you card.

Toy museum
Understanding our past

What you need:

- A range of toys from the past, such as:
  - Wind-up toys
  - Dinky toys (miniature cars)
  - Antique china dolls
  - Dressing up clothes
  - Hoop and stick
  - Old toy telephone
  - Cat's cradle
  - View-Master
  - Rubik's Cube

What to do:

1. Before the activity is due to take place, create a toy museum within the classroom by:
   - Displaying and labelling the toys on tables.
   - Designing an item descriptor for each toy to include: its name, the date the toy was made and instructions on how to play with the toy.
   - Researching, printing out and displaying photographs of children from the period playing with the toys.

2. Encourage the children to explore and ask questions about the toys and the era they came from. Talk to the children about the differences between toys made now and those made in the past.

Top tip

Involve the children's grandparents or older family members by asking the children to bring in photographs, games or stories that are relevant to them. This can then extend into exploring games from other cultures.

What's in it for the children?

The children will begin to learn about their history and about the differences and similarities in the generations who have come before them. They will have the opportunity to explore their heritage and acknowledge the contributions of those generations.

Taking it forward

- Take the children on a visit to a local toy museum to see even more toys and to talk to the experts.

 Health & Safety

Check that the toys are in a suitable condition and cleaned before use.

The pomegranate cake

Food from different cultures

What you need:

- Oven
- 20 cm loose-bottomed cake tin
- Mixing bowl
- Measuring scales
- Wooden spoon
- Skewer
- 200g butter
- 200g caster sugar
- 3 eggs
- Juice ½ lemon
- 240g self-raising flour
- ½ tsp vanilla extract

For the syrup

- Juice ½ lemon
- 2 pomegranates (one juiced, one for seeds)
- 85g caster sugar
- ½ tsp vanilla extract

What to do:

1. Plan how you will support the children in making the cake to take into account your setting and children's ages and abilities. If your setting has a chef you could involve them, alternatively a teacher could lead with a colleague or a parent or carer to support.

2. Explain to the children that they will be making a cake that is special to Azerbaijan, in order to wish a child from Azerbaijan happy birthday. (You could adapt this activity to suit a child in your setting.)

3. Ensure that the children wash their hands.

4. Involve the children in making the cake by giving them tasks such as removing the seeds from the pomegranates, beating the sugar and butter and folding in the flour. The method is as follows:

   - Heat the oven to 160C.
   - Grease and line a 20 cm cake tin.
   - Beat the butter and sugar until pale.
   - Add the eggs one at a time.
   - Add the lemon juice and vanilla extract.
   - Fold in the flour until mixed.
   - Transfer to a cake tin and bake for 50 minutes.
   - Mix the lemon, pomegranate juice, sugar and vanilla.
   - Add the pomegranate seeds.
   - Remove the cake from the oven, poke holes all over with a skewer and pour over the syrup.

Top tip

This activity can be used to celebrate the cultures within your setting by choosing recipes that are relevant to the children and staff.

Health & Safety

Check no one is allergic to pomegranates or any other ingredients used in this cake. Pomegranates contain seeds and children must always be supervised to avoid any choking incidents.

What's in it for the children?

The children are introduced to cuisines from different cultures and ingredients they might not have encountered before. They can develop their own cooking and baking skills, learn to use real tools, understand food science and the effects of heat and time on the ingredients. The children will learn new vocabulary such as sweet, sour, juicy, tangy, flavoursome, aromatic, zesty and jewel-like, and will develop concentration, perseverance and fine motor skills through the act of removing the pomegranate seeds. The children will also develop a sense of accomplishment through achieving something tangible that is bringing so much joy to others.

Taking it forward

- Visit a local market to buy pomegranates and to see the range of foods from different countries.

- Help the children to plan and create a menu from Azerbaijan for the world café (see the activity on page 50).

The colour of me

Celebrating uniqueness and difference

What you need:

- Pastels, crayons, paint, pencils and pens in a range of skin tones, hair and eye colours
- Paper
- Mirrors

Top tip

Visit local art galleries to see how the local community is celebrating diversity through art.

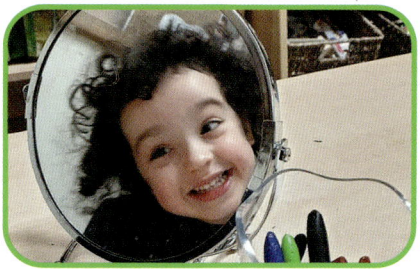

What to do:

1. Set up a table with sufficient paper, mirrors and art materials for each of the children taking part.
2. Explain to the children that they will be making self-portraits to see for themselves and to show others how unique they are. You could create your own self-portrait to share with the children first.
3. Encourage the children to look in the mirror and choose colours that they feel are closest to their own skin, hair and eye colours.
4. Allow the children to experiment with the colours. Support their learning by introducing words that describe the tones and hues of the colours, such as beige, pale, ivory, amber, rose, caramel, chestnut and ebony.

What's in it for the children?

The children will recognise their uniqueness and the uniqueness of others, which encourages inclusion and acceptance. They will also learn how to identify and describe different skin tones, eye and hair colour and will develop their fine motor and drawing skills.

Taking it forward

- The children can help to create a display in their setting and can write or narrate their unique captions to describe their pictures.
- This activity can be extended as a home-learning activity where children can draw their whole family and describe what is unique about each family member.

50 fantastic ideas to encourage diversity and inclusion

Penguins of the world

There is room for us all

What you need:

- An encyclopedia or book about penguins
- Photographs of penguins
- Model penguins (optional)
- An atlas, globe or world map
- Access to the internet (for research)

Top tip

Take the children to the library to look at more books about penguins.

What's in it for the children?

The children will learn about the diversity of penguins that live in different parts of the southern hemisphere and have very different life experiences. This can prompt conversations about there being room on the planet for us all if we are respectful to each other and the world around us. Comparisons can be drawn between the topics explored and the wider context of acceptance.

Taking it forward

- Visit a zoo and talk to the penguin keeper who will be able to tell the children facts about the types of penguins that live there.

Health & Safety

Supervise the children when using toy models as they may have pointed edges.

What to do:

1. This activity can be spread over a week as it is involves a lot of learning.
2. Choose five different species of penguin, for example the Emperor Penguin, the Humboldt Penguin, the Fairy Penguin, the Rockhopper and the African Penguin. Focus on one species per session.
3. Use photographs, models and atlases to teach the children about each of the chosen species. Areas to focus on could include: their habitat, how many eggs the penguins lay, how the penguins look, and where they come from.
4. Using the idea of the different types of penguins, talk to the children about the similarities and differences between people to see if there are any comparisons. For example, some people live in hot countries, some in cold. Expand this area to explore other topics such as appearance and customs.

Celebrating warmth and empathy

The Boy, The Mole, The Fox and The Horse

What you need:

- *The Boy, the Mole, the Fox and the Horse* by Charles Mackesy
- A quiet comfortable space to relax and reflect
- Paper
- Pens, pencils and paint

Top tip

Share this book with the teachers during staff meetings and have a copy in the staff room.

What to do:

1. Read and share *The Boy, the Mole, the Fox and the Horse* with the children.
2. Explore with the children some of the main themes of the book, such as love, friendship, hope and positivity.
3. Ask the children how they feel about the simple drawings.
4. Talk to the children about some of their own experiences of friendship, love and positivity.
5. Following on from these discussions, support the children in creating their own illustrations showing what it is to be kind, brave, caring and so on.
6. Encourage the children to narrate their illustrations, which they can either write down themselves or which can be written down for them by a teacher.
7. Collate all of the illustrations, paintings and stories to create a resource for the nursery.

What's in it for the children?

The children will have an opportunity to describe some of their worries and feelings and to find some of the answers in the uplifting messages in the book. They will be inspired to illustrate and describe their own thoughts and feelings and to share what is important to them. This activity provides a safe space for the children to ask questions and share their own interpretations. In addition to this, the children can see how kindness weaves through our everyday interactions, conversations, actions and thoughts; that kindness does not always mean elaborate gestures, but can mean having a regard for how the other person may be feeling and doing all that can be done to uplift them and cheer them on.

Taking it forward

- The children can plan and role play their own adventures and develop situations where they will need to be supportive, brave and kind towards each other.

Learning about our families

We are all unique

What you need:

- A book about families, such as *The Family Book* by Todd Parr

Top tip ⭐

Provide managerial support to practitioners if required, so that they feel comfortable and confident to answer the children's questions about families in a safe and respectful way.

What to do:

1. Sit a small group of children comfortably and read a story about families together.
2. Allow the children to ask questions whilst you are reading.
3. Look at the pictures of the different families together and ask questions such as, 'Who is in the picture?', 'Where do they live?' and so on.
4. When you have finished the book, encourage the children to share their own experiences of family life by asking them questions such as, 'Who lives in your home with you?', 'Who visits you at home?'

What's in it for the children?

The children will learn that there are many different and diverse types of families. This activity will provide an opportunity to talk about their own families and the families of others and to understand and discuss the differences and similarities between them.

Taking it forward

- Ask parents to share any home experiences and to send in photographs of their families, which can be displayed.

I can be anything

Breaking down gender stereotypes

What you need:

- Card
- A hole punch
- String
- Paints and colouring pens
- Camera (optional)
- Computer and printer

Top tip

Ask parents, carers, grandparents and wider family members to get involved. It's a fun way to learn more about the children's families.

What's in it for the children?

Children will begin to learn that people do a variety of jobs and that jobs are not dependent on gender. This is a fun and creative activity, which introduces new vocabulary and provokes deeper thinking and conversations.

Taking it forward

- Consider adding some interesting props into the role-play area for the children to use as provocations.
- Support the activity by introducing stories, such as *Julian is a Mermaid* by Jessica Love.

What to do:

1. Begin by researching photos of people doing jobs for each letter of the alphabet. For example, an astronaut, a beautician, a carpenter, a diver, and so on. Be sure to include photos that go against gender stereotypes, for example include a male beautician and a female carpenter.
   For example:

   Women:
   - A is for Astronaut
   - B is for Bus driver
   - C is for Carpenter
   - D is for Diver

   Men:
   - A is for Astronaut
   - B is for Beautician
   - C is for Cleaner
   - D is for Dancer

2. Print out the photos and share these with the children. Talk to them about the jobs that their parents, carers and family members do.

3. Ask the children to help make an A to Z book containing the jobs that they would like to do. They can look at the photos for ideas, draw their ideal job or dress up and be photographed in their uniform.

4. Underneath each drawing or photo ask the children to add a sentence about why they would like to do their chosen job. Older children can write their own sentences and younger children can tell the teacher who can write the sentence for them.

5. When the drawings and photos are complete, use the hole punch and string to tie the pages together to create a book.

6. When compiling the book, either choose one profession for each letter, or include multiple examples for each letter to give greater variety.

7. Display the book for the children to look through whenever they like

50 fantastic ideas to encourage diversity and inclusion

Diversity, friendship and kindness

Handa's Surprise

What you need:

- *Handa's Surprise* by Eileen Browne
- The following fruit from the story (either real, plastic, wooden or photos):
  - Banana
  - Guava
  - Orange
  - Mango
  - Pineapple
  - Avocado
  - Passion fruit
- A basket for the fruit

What's in it for the children?

This activity is multi-layered. The children are introduced to worlds outside of their own, and concepts of cultural practices, artefacts and customs. The activity extends language, teaches mathematical sequencing and colour, supports repetition and recall, and builds concentration.

Taking it forward

- Turn the story into a performance.
- For a larger project, look at a world map and find south-west Kenya where the story is set. Plot where the children and their extended families come from in relation to Handa and create a display that can be extended by adding information about each place. This could become a long project across the year.

What to do:

1. Read the story to the children whilst allowing them time to ask questions.
2. Use the fruit to help bring the story to life. Encourage the children to take a lead in this so they are active in the storytelling.
3. After reading the story, talk about south-west Kenya where the story is set. Talk with the children about the similarities and differences between what they see in the story and where they live.

Top tip

Gather together some pictures of Kenya and the animals that live there to share with the children whilst reading the story.

➕ Health & Safety

Check for allergies before doing any food-related activities.

Exploring our feelings

Taking inspiration from *Giraffes Can't Dance*

What you need:

- *Giraffes Can't Dance* by Giles Andreae
- A toy giraffe (optional)
- Space to dance
- A range of music
- Paper and pens

Top tip

As a further extension to the task, support the children in writing letters to Gerald and his friends inviting them to their dance.

What to do:

1. Read *Giraffes Can't Dance* to the children.
2. Ask the children questions to seek their opinions about Gerald's situation, such as 'Why did Gerald think he was bad at dancing?', 'Why does Gerald feel sad that he can't dance?', 'Should Gerald feel sad?', 'Does it matter if Gerald can't dance?'
3. Using the toy giraffe as a prop, ask the children to describe his feelings. Use the opportunity to introduce the children to new vocabulary, such as brave, timid, confident, sensitive, anxious.
4. Support the children in exploring the feelings discussed using their body movements and facial expressions, as well as words.
5. Conclude the activity by dancing with the children in order to share in Gerald's celebration.
6. Encourage the children to create their own dance moves to teach to their friends.

What's in it for the children?

This is a fun activity where the children will begin to develop a sense of empathy through learning new vocabulary to describe feelings. They can be introduced to a new range of music whilst being active and strengthening their gross motor skills through dancing.

Taking it forward

- Blend music and feelings by introducing the children to a range of different music. Focus on one piece of music at a time and then ask the children how the music makes them feel. Possible genres could include: classical, jazz, marching band, folk, county. The list is endless!
- End each activity with a dance.

Fingerprints
Our unique passwords

What you need:

- Softened air-drying clay
- Calcium carbonate powder for dusting
- Sticky tape
- Small brushes
- Magnifying glasses

Top tip ⭐

Make a fingerprint book containing comments from each of the children about their fingerprints.

What's in it for the children?

The children will be shown that although we all have fingers, our fingerprints are unique to us. It will also be an opportunity for the children to take part in a simple science activity.

Taking it forward

- The children can take some clay home and take fingerprints of their family members.

➕ Health & Safety

Check for any allergies before sharing the clay or calcium carbonate powder with the children.

What to do:

1. Before starting the activity, set up a scientific laboratory for the children to make casts of their fingerprints. This should include (softened) clay divided up into pieces large enough to press a thumb or finger into, magnifying glasses, brushes and a piece of sticky tape to press on the print and lift.

2. Introduce the activity by talking to the children about fingerprints, exploring their different shapes and patterns. Encourage the children to look at their own and each other's fingerprints.

3. Discuss how fingerprints are all unique in the same way that we are all unique.

4. Support the children to firmly press their thumb or finger into the clay.

5. Show the children how to use the magnifying glasses to examine their fingerprints.

6. Leave the clay to dry and then support the children to dust their fingerprints with some calcium carbonate powder to emphasise the patterns. The children can then re-examine their fingerprints.

Baby you're fantastic!

Looking at similarities and differences

What you need:

- Baby photos of the children
- A mirror for each of the children

Top tip

Use the children's baby photos to create a collage display.

What's in it for the children?

The children will learn how they are unique, but they will also be able to see that they share some characteristics with their peers, thus showing that they are different but also the same. The children will also begin to understand that physical changes take place as we age.

Taking it forward

- Make a card game of the photos so the children can play 'Baby Snap' and spot themselves and their friends.

- Ask members of staff to bring in their baby photos to see if the children can guess who is who. The children can then list the similarities and differences between the teachers as babies and adults.

- Use the opportunity to introduce some simple science by explaining how babies grow from a tiny egg.

What to do:

1. Write and send an email or post a notice on the parents and carers' information board to invite them to send in photos of their children as babies; these can be physical photos or electronic versions that are emailed to the setting. Explain that the aim of the activity is to use the photos to examine similarities and differences between how their children looked as babies and how they look now.

2. If possible, make copies of the photos so that they can be put on display as well as being used for the activity.

3. Give each child their baby photo and a mirror. Invite them to look at their photos focusing on their unique features, such as skin, hair and eye colour, face shape and so on. Ask them to look in the mirror and identify what is different now that they are older.

4. Encourage descriptive language to describe facial features. Keep a note of the words the children use to add to any display that you design.

5. Put the children into pairs and invite them to compare their photos, picking out the differences and similarities between each other.

6. Bring the children back together in one group. Discuss with them what differences and similarities they found.

50 fantastic ideas to encourage diversity and inclusion

What's in the box?

Teaching babies Makaton

What you need:

- A box with a lid
- A range of objects such as:
  - A ball
  - A bell
  - A toy animal
  - A book
  - A spoon
  - A cup
  - A comb
  - A toy brick
- The Makaton signs, available from: www.makaton.org
- A comfortable space

Top tip

Repeat this activity frequently, as babies need repetition to consolidate their learning.

What's in it for the children?

The babies will learn what to expect once the practitioner starts singing the song. The anticipation of the lifting of the lid will engage the babies and build concentration and listening skills. The element of surprise and the adults enjoying the activity is a great joy for babies.

Taking it forward

- For older babies, choose different objects to place inside the box and ask them to replace the lid on the box.

✚ Health & Safety

Babies must be supervised at all times. One of the main ways that babies learn is by putting objects in their mouths, so please be alert.

What to do:

1. Sit a small group of babies comfortably in your chosen space.
2. Choose one baby to start the activity.
3. Sing the following lines starting with the baby's name to the tune of 'The Farmer's Wife' nursery rhyme. Whilst singing, use the Makaton signs to accompany the words:

   What's in the box?

   What's in the box?

   Tell me, show me, what's in the box?

4. Open the box lid and narrate the activity as you do so: '*What have we got in the box, ooh what could it be?*'. Slowly bring the object out of the box so that the babies are all watching.
5. Ensure all the babies have a turn.
6. When all babies have had a turn, close the lid to demonstrate the end of the activity.

Time machine

Understanding my past

What you need:

- Examples of time machines collected from books or the internet
- Cardboard to make the time machine
- Paint, pens and crayons
- Decorations
- Cards and envelopes

Top tip ⭐

Make a time machine book with quotes from families and staff.

What to do:

1. Introduce the idea of the past to the children; go back as far as you want – the dinosaurs is often a good reference point!
2. Talk about the similarities and differences between things in the past and now.
3. Explain to the children that they are going to create a time machine and then they will write invitations to the people they would like to join them in the time machine.
4. Show the children examples of time machines.
5. Prepare a big space to make the machine.
6. Design and create the machine with the children.
7. Invite the children to think about who they would like to take in the time machine and why.
8. Make a list of who will be accompanying the children and why.
9. Create invitation cards with the children.

What's in it for the children?

The children will begin to understand the concept of the past and the differences and similarities between the past and now. This will help the children to realise that things often change and that this is a good thing, thus reducing their fear of change and allowing them to accept different ways of doing things. Through talking about who they would like to take with them in the time machine, the children can begin to think about the people who are important to them and why. In addition, physical and creative skills are developed.

Taking it forward

- The children can interview their teachers and family members regarding who they would like in their time machine and why.

Pen pals
Making new friends

What you need:

- Card
- Paper
- Pencils
- Stamps
- Envelopes
- Addresses for chosen pen pals

Top tip ⭐

Take the children on a trip to the post box or even the post office.

What's in it for the children?

The children will be able to make new friends with people outside their immediate world through the medium of writing. They will learn about the experiences of others and develop a sense of empathy. The activity also develops fine motor and mark making skills when writing the letters.

Taking it forward

- Make links with a nursery in a different area of the country so that the children can write to other children from different areas and backgrounds.

➕ Health & Safety

For safeguarding purposes, only forenames should be used in correspondence between the children and their pen pals.

What to do:

1. Prior to the activity, contact a local elderly care home to enquire if they would like to take part in a pen pal activity. If they agree, ask them to send a list of names of those residents who would like to take part.
2. Write each 'pen pal' name on a piece of card.
3. Talk to the children about pen pals. Explain that they will write to a pen pal who will write back to them.
4. Talk about some of the things they might tell their pen pal about themselves and the questions they might ask.
5. Give out the cards with the names of the care home residents to the children.
6. Support the children in writing to their pen pals. This will need planning and modelling for the children so that they know what to write.
7. When the letters have been written, put them in envelopes and then in a larger envelope addressed to the care home. It would be helpful to write a covering note to accompany the cards and letters.

Would you like to be our Pen Pal?

Careers fair

Challenging stereotypes

What you need:

- Space within your setting to set up the activity and a range of props that relate to any given profession, for example, if setting up a grocery store, items could include:
  - Vegetables and fruits (real if possible for a better learning resource)
  - Canned food
  - Dry goods
  - Cash registers
  - Play money
  - Magazines
  - Shopping baskets

Top tip

Use recycled paper and newspapers to make uniforms to extend the role play and make props.

What to do:

This activity can take place over a number of weeks to allow sufficient time to explore and embed the activity.

1. Each week set up a space as a workshop that focuses on a profession. For example, a builders' yard, a doctor's surgery, a grocery store, a blacksmith, a garden centre, an architects' office, a space centre (the list is endless).

2. Start week one with a grocery store. Set up the learning space with the items that you have gathered for the activity.

3. Encourage the children to role play in order to experience what it is like to work in a grocery store. Support the children to take turns at serving and being served.

4. Help the children to understand how to deal with transactions by working out the costs of items and using money to pay and give or receive change.

5. Observe what roles the boys and girls are naturally drawn to and consciously encourage the children to try all roles. This is particularly powerful when dealing with careers that are often gender stereotyped.

What's in it for the children?

The children will experience a diverse variety of job roles and in so doing are encouraged to challenge gender stereotypes by taking part in every activity. These activities provide an opportunity for the children to understand the importance of each job role and how they themselves can make a positive contribution to society when they grow up.

Taking it forward

- Invite parents, carers and / or members of the local community to come in and talk to the children about their professions.

50 fantastic ideas to encourage diversity and inclusion

I baked a cake for Christmas

Supporting bilingual children

What you need:

- A big mixing bowl and a wooden spoon
- Chefs' hats made by the children (optional)

What to do:

1. Sit with the children in a circle.
2. Start by holding the mixing bowl and wooden spoon.
3. Introduce the game by passing the bowl to the child sat next to you and asking them to start the game by repeating after you: 'I baked a cake for Christmas and in it I put…'. They should then add the name of the ingredient that they would like to include in the mixture. Remind the children that the ingredient can be anything at all.
4. When the child has said their ingredient, ask them to stir the imaginary mixture in the bowl and pass it to the child sat next to them.
5. Ask the child who receives the bowl to say the phrase 'I baked a cake for Christmas and in it I put …' and then repeat the ingredient from the first child before adding their own ingredient and stirring the imaginary mixture.
6. The bowl is then passed from child to child, with the list of ingredients growing each time.
7. If a child does not have the vocabulary to come up with their own ingredient, ensure that you support them before the activity begins by using visual aids to practise a word that they would like to use.
8. If a child forgets the list, the group can help them to recall the ingredients, making it a fun and inclusive activity.
9. This sequence is repeated around the circle until all of the children have had a turn.

Top tip

The theme does not have to be 'Christmas'; it can be any event that is important and meaningful to the children, for example birthdays, other religious festivals and so on.

What's in it for the children?

This activity is a good opportunity for bilingual children to practise their vocabulary and for all children to develop their public speaking in a safe and small group. In addition to this, the children will be able to develop their language and memory recall. Each child's contribution is important and vital to the game and the children will have a lot of fun working together to achieve results. The activity will also provide an opportunity for the children to understand the importance of each other's views, opinions and choices whilst showing patience and practising taking turns.

50 fantastic ideas to encourage diversity and inclusion

Taking it forward

- This game could be played with families at home with older siblings and grandparents. It can also be played on long journeys where the whole family can join in, providing an opportunity to replace the use of electronic devices to keep the children entertained.

- Support the children to make a recipe book with the ingredients they listed and go on an outing to the shop to buy them.

- Create an opportunity for some messy play by adding a few real ingredients to the bowl, such as flour, sugar and water.

My space
Time to reset

What you need:

- A small space in the room
- Several large pieces of material in calm and neutral colours
- Furniture to support the material
- Bulldog clips
- Items to make the space inviting, such as:
  - Battery operated fairy lights in calming colours
  - Large hula hoops with pieces of multi-textured ribbons attached
  - A basket filled with homemade books about each child and their families
  - Soft cushions
  - Some small blankets

What's in it for the children?

Children are often expected to negotiate, take turns and be around other peers of similar ages and temperaments; it can be exhausting managing their own feelings, caring and empathising with others and being sociable all of the time. This activity provides children with an opportunity to take a few minutes out to recalibrate and reset. This activity can also support children with special educational needs who at times may find the nursery environment over stimulating and may enjoy having their own familiar space to feel in control of their feelings.

Taking it forward

- Add multi-sensory resources in response to observing how the children use the space.

What to do:

1. Create a den for the children either by using a small space in the room or the space under a table.
2. Attach the large piece of material to the sides of the furniture to create a ceiling for the den and secure it with the bulldog clips.
3. Add privacy by attaching some additional material to hang down.
4. Make the space cosy and inviting by using the selection of items that have been gathered.
5. Place the hula hoops with the textured ribbons inside the den. These can be used to visually create space by those children who are struggling to connect with others.
6. Observe the children's emotions and how they use language when in the den. Wait to be invited into the children's play.

✚ Health & Safety

Check in regularly with the children to make sure that they are safe and use light coloured materials for the den so the children can also be seen from the outside. Always check that the lights are in safe working order and that the batteries do not pose a choking hazard.

Top tip ⭐

Keep this space decluttered and calm.

Communication generation

Comparing the past to now

What you need:

- A range of items that are used as a means of communication. These should be from the past and the present, such as:
  - A telephone
  - A telegram
  - A television
  - Makaton signs
  - Letters
  - Emails
  - Text messages
  - Photos of homing pigeons and smoke signals
  - Examples of hieroglyphics
- Also:
  - Paper
  - Pencils

What to do:

1. Talk to the children about the need for people to communicate with each other. Ask questions such as, 'Why do we communicate?', 'What would happen if we didn't communicate?', 'How does it make you feel when you communicate with your family and friends?'.

2. Explain how over the centuries human beings have communicated with each other by using a variety of different methods and tools.

3. Explore with the children each of the items you have collected. Encourage the children to try to guess how items from the past were used as a means of communication.

4. Make comparisons between the ways in which people communicated in the past and how we communicate today.

5. Support the children to write some words using hieroglyphs or to write a short letter to a member of their family.

Top tip

Ask the children about the ways in which they communicate with their family and friends.

What's in it for the children?

The children will learn that there are many ways in which we can communicate with each other. The children will also begin to understand that communication varies between different cultures and in different communities, and that communication has changed a great deal over time. This activity is also an opportunity for the children to appreciate the modern world in which we live.

Taking it forward

- Focus on a particular country or culture to learn about different languages and the different ways in which people across the world communicate with one another.

The friendship quilt

A collaborative art project

What you need:

- A white square of felt for each child
- A hole punch
- Pens in a range of colours including a selection of skin tones
- Children's plastic needles and thin string

Top tip ⭐

Display the friendship quilt in the entrance to the setting.

What to do:

1. Ask each child to take a felt square and draw a picture of their friend. They may choose to draw themselves with their friends.

2. Offer the children a range of skin-toned pens and help them to match their own or their friend's skin, hair and eye colours.

3. Whilst the children are working on their drawings, ask each child 'What is friendship?' and 'Why is friendship important?' and record their responses. Use these comments in speech bubbles or labels when displaying the project. Keep a diary of the progress and note down the comments in the diary.

4. When the children have completed their drawings, punch a hole along each of the sides of the felt square.

5. Lay each felt square out on a flat surface to form a large collage.

6. Support the children in sewing the squares together through the pre-punched holes, using a needle and thread.

7. When all of the pieces are joined together, hang the quilt on the wall to display the children's friendship.

8. Spread the drawing and sewing project out across the term to ensure that the topic is explored in detail.

✚ Health & Safety

Closely supervise the use of the plastic sewing needles.

What's in it for the children?

The children will develop their personal, social and emotional understanding by exploring the concept of friendship through discussions and with the support of an adult helping to narrate their learning. The children will learn to work collaboratively as each individually crafted square forms a whole. Sewing will also strengthen the children's fine motor skills.

Taking it forward

- Make this an ongoing project; when a new child joins the setting encourage them to add a square to the quilt.

- Add quotes or photos about friendship to the quilt.

50 fantastic ideas to encourage diversity and inclusion

The card factory

Celebrating special events

What you need:

- A box (for resources)
- Card and paper
- Pens and crayons
- Recycled and repurposed decorations, such as ribbons, buttons, bows, scraps of material, leftover wrapping paper or wallpaper, pictures from magazines, leaves and flowers
- Glue and scissors
- Envelopes

What's in it for the children?

The children can learn about special events and occasions that they themselves may not celebrate and in so doing begin to understand what is important to their friends. They can learn to write messages with a purpose and understand how sending a message can be an important way to celebrate an occasion. In addition to this, the children will practise their fine motor skills through using scissors to cut materials, decorating and writing in their cards.

Taking it forward

- Create a relationship with a local care home. In agreement with the care home, children could send letters and cards, developing their empathy skills and their understanding of how we care for others. See 'Pen pals' on page 31.

⊕ Health & Safety

Supervise the children at all times when using small items and scissors.

What to do:

1. Decide with the children the event that that they will make a card for; this could be an upcoming festival that a child in the setting will be celebrating, a birthday or a religious occasion.
2. Ask them to choose who they will send their card to.
3. Invite the children to choose from the resources that are available in the box.
4. Help the children to make cards and write a simple message and their name inside. Support younger children by asking them to tell you the message, which can then be written for them.
5. Show the children how to put their cards in envelopes.

Top tip

Involve the children in the planning aspect of this activity.

50 fantastic ideas to encourage diversity and inclusion

Let's play with my favourite toy

Learning to play together

What you need:

- A range of toys such as:
  - Trains
  - Dolls
  - Blocks
  - Balls
  - Cars
  - A marble game
  - Chalk boards

Top tip ⭐

Consider the quiet child who may need a little more support to engage and feel part of the activity. Talk to them about their favourite toys through a storytelling session or observing play and then carefully select some of the toys they like to add to the collection.

What's in it for the children?

Children will begin to understand how they can play with each other. They will learn how to use a toy as a way of joining a game and connecting with and considering the feelings of others.

Taking it forward

- Put the children into pairs and ask them to create a new game together using two different toys.

- Put two pairs of children together and ask them to tell each other about their games.

What to do:

1. Find a quiet carpet space and display a selection of toys from across the nursery.
2. Invite the children to choose their favourite toy.
3. Settle them comfortably within a circle.
4. Ask the children, in turn, why they like their toys.
5. Ask them to identify which of their friends' toys they would also like to play with.
6. Ask the children to think of a game that would involve all of the toys that they could play together; use prompts if necessary, such as an item from a game the children know or a clue to start them thinking.

The book hospital

Looking after books in need of repair

What you need:

- Some old books in need of repair
- A box in which to store the books
- A 'repair kit' containing items such as child-appropriate sewing needles and string, sticky tape, staplers, a hole punch and sticky back plastic

Top tip

Use the book hospital during quieter times as an activity where the practitioner supports individuals or small groups of children to repair books.

What to do:

1. Introduce the book box to the children during circle time.
2. Talk to them about the importance of looking after our books. Explain why reading books is fun and invite the children to talk about their favourite books and characters.
3. Introduce the idea of kindness. Tell the children a story about a group of children who are sad because their books are torn. Tell the children how books are made and what can happen when we don't take care of them.
4. Show the children some of the ripped or broken books and ask them to consider what repairs might need to be made.
5. Show the children how they can repair the books by inserting the sewing needle and thread along the seam and stitching a line which needs to be fastened off with a double stitch. Use the hole punch to create holes for inserting the sewing needle, if necessary.
6. Introduce new words such as 'adhesive', 'spine', 'binding', 'margins' and 'stitching'.
7. Celebrate together when the books have been mended and thank the children for being kind!

Health & Safety

If children are using tools they must be supervised at all times.

What's in it for the children?

The children are introduced to the concept of kindness, by learning to take responsibility for mending and repairing instead of consuming and discarding. They will begin to develop an understanding of how we need to care for things that bring us joy. The children will also develop their fine motor skills, as well as learning about perseverance, concentration and problem-solving.

Taking it forward

- Suggest that the children repair their books at home.

- Take photos of the activity to display.

- If a book is beyond repair, repurpose it by making a storybook collage or favourite character puppets.

Sofa talk

Nurturing conversations

What you need:

- A sofa or a cosy space
- Cushions
- Flowers and/or plants
- A selection of books
- Cuddly toys
- Soft music

What to do:

1. Create a cosy space using some or all of the items listed. Ensure that the area is inviting, free from clutter and comfortable.
2. This space can be permanently available to the children to use for their enjoyment and to spend time talking with their friends.
3. Encourage the children to use the space by sitting and waiting for them to join to talk with you.
4. Encourange the children to empathise and offer advice if others share their experiences.

Top tip

Children often express their worries through their monster stories. Work through these with the children, don't just ignore them.

What's in it for the children?

The children can form secure friendships and begin to learn to listen to each other. The conversations the children have can provide an opportunity to share experiences and to offer advice, all of which can help to develop empathy. In these situations, children will often develop role play scenarios to act out their experiences, which allows them to work through their worries and to find solutions together. This activity is particularly effective for new or shy children who may struggle to voice their opinions or share their thoughts in a larger group.

Taking it forward

- Develop projects based around any trends that appear. For example, if a child is showing anxiety about going to school, teachers can plan meaningful activities around starting school.
- Involve parents and carers by talking to them to let them know what is happening with their children.

✚ Health & Safety

Remain vigilant and sensitive to the children's needs and be mindful that a child may disclose something that requires reporting. If such a situation does occur, follow the setting's safeguarding procedures.

Thank you cards

Random acts of kindness

What you need:

- A selection of card folded in half to make cards
- Envelopes
- Glue
- Paint
- Pens
- Ribbon
- Environmentally friendly glitter
- Decorations

Top tip ⭐

Kindness is contagious!

What to do:

1. Explain that it makes people feel happy when others are kind to them. Ask the children for examples of how others have made them happy by being kind.
2. Introduce the idea of making cards to say 'thank you'.
3. Suggest that the children think of someone who always helps them – this can be a parent or carer, a relative, a teacher, a shop keeper, a cleaner, a bus driver – the list can be very long!
4. Hand out the pre-folded card to the children and support them in writing their message.
5. Model the writing for the children. Suggest they start with one of the following sentences: 'Thank you for always...', 'I am really happy that you...', 'I wanted to say thank you for...'.
6. When the children have completed their writing, support them in decorating the front of their cards.
7. When the cards are finished, the children can give them to the people they would like to thank.

What's in it for the children?

The children will begin to understand the importance of kindness and will learn to become more empathetic.

Taking it forward

- Get involved in World Kindness Day (www.mentalhealth.org. uk/publications/doing-good-does-you-good/random-acts-kindness), Random Acts of Kindess Day (www. randomactsofkindness.org/rak-day) and the Empathy Lab (www. empathylab.uk).

The message tree

Expressing feelings

What you need:

- A small tree; either an indoor plant or a tree made from branches or wood
- Pens
- Paper pre-cut into leaf shapes
- Laminating pouches
- A hole punch
- Ribbon

Top tip

Tune into the children and create activities based on their messages.

What to do:

1. Set up the activity with the pre-cut paper leaves and pens.
2. Explain to the children that they can write messages on the leaves and that they can then tie them onto the tree.
3. Encourage the children to write or draw their personal messages. Guide the children by sharing examples, such as 'I miss Mummy', 'I like my Granny's house', 'I am going to be 4', 'My baby is coming from my mummy's tummy'.
4. Provide the necessary support and scaffolding. Messages can be in any form of mark making, from scribbles with the adult annotating to a hand-written note.
5. When the children have finished writing or drawing their messages, laminate the paper leaves and punch a hole in the top.
6. Help the children to tie their leaves to the tree.
7. Read one or two messages every day and ask the children if they would like to think more about the messages. These can be explored through other activities, such as story time and role play.

What's in it for the children?

The children are given an opportunity to write a range of ideas, comments and observations, and to consider the ideas and feelings of others. Their sense of achievement and self-worth is also increased when their messages are read out. This activity also provides opportunities for the children to mark make and write for a purpose.

Taking it forward

- Provide children with blank leaf-shaped paper to take home with them so that they can write and share messages with family and friends.

Empathy day
Walking in someone else's shoes

What you need:

- **Access to a computer for research**

Top tip

Let parents and carers know about your forthcoming Empathy Day so that they can share in the celebration.

What to do:

1. Visit the EmpathyLab website (www.empathylab.uk) to confirm the date for Empathy Day.
2. Each year the website provides a link with activities and ideas for the day, with a summary of the countdown, the day itself and how to access free community toolkits.
3. Use the website's free resources, book and story recommendations to help you plan the day.
4. Possible activities could include the 'mirror body language game' whereby the teacher puts a scowl on his or her face and asks 'Am I cross?' and then a smile and asks 'Am I happy?'.

What's in it for the children?

The children learn about empathy and kindness in an open and flexible way. This is also a very soft introduction to the bigger concept of sustainability. Staff can use the 17 Sustainable Development Goals to begin to think more broadly about how we are kind to each other, nature and our local environment, and what we might do to better understand the world from another person's perspective. For example, ask the children about how we can help a child who does not have enough food or clothes. Or take them on a walk around their local neighbourhood and identify ways of making it feel safer, such as by doing a litter pick or planting a tree.

Taking it forward

- Take the children on an Empathy Walk – a short walk around your neighbourhood where you ask the children to imagine themselves in the place of the people that they see. For example a homeless person or two people having fun. Ask the children how it makes them feel when they see these people; happy, worried, angry and so on.

The zoo in our garden

Being kind to our environment

What you need:

- A garden, outdoor space or window box
- Plants
- Materials to make bird feeders
- Materials to make a bird bath
- A bug hotel
- A bug catcher

Top tip

Encourage the staff to be brave and not only allow the children to explore the creatures they find but to explore with them.

What to do:

1. This is a large project that can be broken up into different activities.

2. Support the children in creating a nature-friendly environment either in the nursery garden, outdoor space or in window boxes. This can include activities such as planting flowers and shrubs, building a log or rock pile, making a bird bath out of a recycled container or upturned dustbin lid, and creating a compost heap.

3. Build or purchase a bug hotel to encourage insects. This can then form the basis of teaching the children about the life cycles of insects.

4. Using a bug catcher, catch bugs and examine them in detail before releasing them back into nature.

5. Sign up to the RSPB teaching resources (www.rspb.org.uk/fun-and-learning/for-teachers/lesson-plans-and-supporting-resources/) and build a bird-spotting space in the setting with equipment such as binoculars, reference cards and a clipboard and pencil.

6. See *50 Fantastic Ideas for Nursery Gardens* for more ideas.

What's in it for the children?

Children will learn to be respectful and empathetic to bugs and insects and nature as a whole. These activities also give scope to teach the importance of finding ways to live together as every creature, no matter how small, has a place on the planet.

Taking it forward

- Extend the children's interests by looking up the creatures in books and on the internet and discovering fun facts to take home and share with families.

Health & Safety

Ensure that the children wash their hands after touching anything that is used in the activity. Check for allergic reactions; some plants can cause a skin rash.

World café

Exploration through food

What you need:

- A table and chairs
- A tablecloth
- A tea set
- A range of magazines with images of different people and places
- Flowers
- Music
- A world map or globe
- A computer for research
- Paper, pencils and crayons

Top tip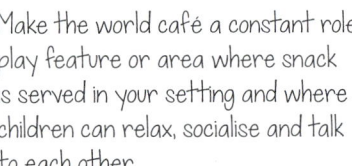

Make the world café a constant role play feature or area where snack is served in your setting and where children can relax, socialise and talk to each other.

What to do:

1. Explain to the children that they are going to create a café that will serve food and drink from around the world.
2. Show the children the resources for the café and let them take the lead in setting it up.
3. Using the globe or map ask the children to choose a country that they would like to visit.
4. Research this country with the children to learn about the food and customs. Encourage questions and conversations.
5. Model different menus for the children and support them to create their own menus using the information they have found about the food from their chosen country.
6. When the menus have been created and the café set up, the children can take turns at serving and being served.
7. Each week, look at the globe or map with the children and choose a different county to visit. Research this country and create a new menu.

World Cafe

What's in it for the children?

This activity provides an opportunity to learn about different countries, cuisines and customs. It is also a good opportunity for the children to explore a safe space where they can make friends, talk to each other and develop their social skills, such as active listening, negotiating and learning the art of conversation.

Taking it forward

- Plan visits to local cafés that offer a range of different cuisines.

Health & Safety

Check the food served in the café is suitable for children with food allergies, intolerances and specific dietary requirements.

Parachute fun

Playing collaboratively

What you need:

- A parachute
- A large space, either indoors or outdoors

Top tip

Prepare the parachute activity by having a children's planning meeting where issues of access, fairness and ensuring everyone's participation can be explored.

What's in it for the children?

This activity helps the children to learn how to play games cooperatively and supports their ability to show empathy to those who are less able to follow instructions or complete physical tasks. The children will learn how to follow directions and instructions, to work as part of a team and to wait and take their turn.

Taking it forward

- Introduce the children to rhythm and rhyme by adding music and poems during the games.

- Develop the children's language and social skills by telling stories and singing songs together during the games.

- Discuss with the children ways of ensuring everyone can participate.

✚ Health & Safety

Make sure there is enough space for the children to stand around the parachute.

What to do:

1. Place the children in a circle and invite them to hold the parachute. Give them clear instructions on how to hold the parachute.

2. Ensure that the children have enough space between them so that they do not bump into each other.

3. When the children are comfortable in their positions, join the circle.

4. Introduce the game that you want to play and explain how each child gets a turn. Two possible games are:

   - The mushroom game. Ask the children to spread the parachute out evenly, holding their own section tightly. Then ask them to pull the parachute down to their knees and on the magic word 'mushroom' pull it upwards without letting go. As the air fills the parachute the shape becomes like a mushroom.

   - Move like a dinosaur. Ask the children to spread the parachute out evenly, holding their own section tightly. Ask them to raise the parachute up and down like the flapping wings of a Pterodactyl. Then ask the children to raise the parachute as high as they can like an Allosaurus. Finally, shake the parachute rapidly like the tail of a Stegosaurus.

Football

Encouraging teamwork

What you need:

- A playground or large indoor space
- A whistle
- Different coloured bibs
- Goal posts
- A handmade trophy

Top tip

To avoid conflict, encourage the children to give lots of praise, to be enthusiastic about the game and to cheer each other along.

What's in it for the children?

The children will gain an understanding of teamwork, team spirit and the importance of working together to achieve a common goal. Played fairly, games can build confidence and help children to understand the importance of taking part, gracefully accepting defeat and relishing in the other team's victory. The children will develop an understanding of the game, simple rules and will have fun whilst keeping active.

Taking it forward

- Read books about playing football.
- Explore the diversity within the world's football teams, for example women's football teams, disabled teams and mixed teams.
- Invite parents and carers to coach or share their football skills with the children.
- Contact other local nurseries and set up a 'nursery world cup' tournament.

What to do:

1. Divide the children into four teams (A, B, C and D). If possible, ensure that the children are a similar age.
2. Help the children to agree a team name and nominate a captain for each team.
3. Explain in simple terms the importance of each player and each position within the team.
4. The teams will compete in a simple four-team round-robin tournament as follows:

    Round 1: A vs B and C vs D

    Round 2: B vs D and A vs C

    Round 3: D vs A and B vs C

5. Play short games and blow the whistle to start and end the games.
6. Record the number of goals scored for each of the teams during each of the matches.
7. At the end of the tournament, the team with the highest score wins.
8. Present the winning team with the handmade trophy.

✚ Health & Safety

Ensure a first aid kit is on hand as there is potential for falling over, bumping into each other and getting hit by the ball.

Jigsaw

We all fit together

What you need:

- A large piece of card
- A4 card or paper (make sure that each piece is identical in size and colour)
- Pencils, colouring pencils, crayons and pens
- Glue stick
- Laminator and laminating pouches
- A camera
- A printer

Top tip

Photocopy the children's work and use the copies to make the puzzles so that the children can take their masterpieces home.

What's in it for the children?

The children learn that every piece of a puzzle is needed to complete the whole and can begin to understand how this is also the case with people – we are all different but all equally important.

Taking it forward

- The children can describe their individual pictures and make up stories, which can lead to more projects around the topics they share.

What to do:

1. Give each child a piece of A4 paper or card.
2. Ask them to draw a picture of themselves.
3. Collect all of the pictures and lay them side by side on top of the large piece of card. Glue the pictures onto the card.
4. Take a photograph of the drawing to later show the children the completed jigsaw.
5. Turn the drawing over and draw a jigsaw pattern on the back of the card.
6. Cut out the jigsaw pieces and laminate them for longevity.
7. Jumble the pieces up so that they are not in sequential order.
8. Using the photograph as their guide, support the children in putting the puzzle back together again.
9. When the puzzle is back together again, talk to the children about the way in which they are like a puzzle – they are all different, but they all fit together as a team and every one of them is important for the team to be complete.

Helicopter

The power of planned story time

What you need:

- Some floor space
- A blue mat or tape
- A sheet of paper
- A pen
- Two adults
- A stick that, when held, denotes the speaker (optional)

Top tip ⭐

Consider how you support the storytelling and drama process so that no child is left out. Take a little extra time to support children with language delays, bilingual children or shy children, but manage this so the flow of the story continues.

What to do:

1. Ask six children to sit comfortably in a circle.
2. Use the blue mat or tape to mark out a space, which becomes the drama space.
3. Introduce the activity to the children. They will be making a story which they will then act out.
4. Remind the children that a story has a beginning, a middle and an end.
5. Involving the children, decide what the story will be about and talk about some possible ideas that they could include.
6. Explain that they will build the story with one child beginning and the others adding to the story, but that each child has a turn.
7. Follow the pattern of the circle. Use a talking stick (whereby the child holding the stick talks and the others listen) if helpful to focus on the child who is speaking.
8. Record the story, which is best kept to one page.
9. When every child has had a turn, read the story back to the children.
10. Support the children in acting the story out.

What's in it for the children?

This collaborative activity helps the children to understand that everyone has a chance to contribute while everyone else has to listen, therefore demonstrating that everyone's opinions are important. The children will also learn how stories work whilst developing new descriptive vocabulary.

Taking it forward

- Print the story out and create a display. Use captions and photos to show parents and carers how the children use their imaginations to create their stories. These stories will also demonstrate their world views.

Fire lighting
We are not scared

What you need:

- A lighter
- A metal container
- Newspapers
- Dry twigs
- A bucket of water
- A wet towel
- A bucket of dirt
- A fire extinguisher
- Marshmallows (optional)

Top tip

Invite a parent or carer with experience of a fire pit to volunteer.

What's in it for the children?

The children will begin to understand about the world in which they live whilst being taught to respect nature and appreciate how it can help us. It is also an opportunity for the children to do something brave together and learn to be kind and supportive to those who are more fearful.

Taking it forward

- Take the children to visit the local fire station where they can learn more about fire safety whilst feeling a sense of being part of the community.

✚ Health & Safety

Ensure you complete a risk assessment and share this with parents and carers prior to the activity. Work with small groups of children and ensure that fire safety equipment, such as water, wet towels and a fire extinguisher, are to hand.

What to do:

1. Introduce the activity to the children during circle time and stress the importance of keeping safe by listening to the instructions.
2. Prepare the pit by layering paper and wood kindling (collect twigs for kindling with the children in advance of the activity).
3. Narrate the process throughout so that the children can understand what is happening whilst extending their vocabulary.
4. Sit the children at a suitable distance away from the fire so that they will not be hit by flying sparks.
5. Light the fire.
6. Sing campfire songs, which can be learnt in preparation for the activity, and toast marshmallows.
7. When the activity is completed, let the fire burn out and then slowly add water to cool it down.

Games from different cultures

Mancala

What you need:

- Mancala the board game or a homemade version using:
  - 12 egg cups or small bowls
  - Stones, pompoms, small blocks or buttons (the game requires four items in each egg cup/bowl, but this can be reduced to make the game easier for children)

Top tip ⭐

The game can be played with chalks on the floor or can be drawn on a piece of paper, and any materials can be used instead of stones.

What's in it for the children?

The children will learn a game from another culture. Mancala can be traced back to ancient Egypt and ancient Sudan and Ghana but is now popular all over Africa, the Middle East, the Caribbean and the US. This is also an opportunity for the children to learn early mathematics skills such as subitizing (the ability to identify a small set of numbers quickly without actually counting). In addition to this, the children will learn patience and perseverance and will enjoy spending time with an adult or a skilful peer where they can problem-solve together. This is an opportunity to learn how to win and lose graciously.

Taking it forward

- Ask parents and carers for games from their homes. Where necessary adapt them to fit with the children's learning and development stages.

What to do:

1. Select two players.
2. Place four stones into each bowl, except the long bowls at each end because these (the Mancalas) are where the winning stones are collected.
3. Place the board between the players, ensuring that the Mancalas are positioned with each player playing one side. Each player's own Mancala is on their right side.
4. The first player picks up the stones from one of the small sections on their side and starts to count them out as they place one stone in every bowl, including their own Mancala.
5. Once the player has placed each stone their turn is over, except if their last stone ends in the Mancala. In which case they have another go.
6. If the player reaches the other player's Mancala they should skip this and continue in the small bowls, including the other player's side until all the stones have finished.
7. If the player drops their last stone in one of their own empty bowls, but there are stones in their opponent's bowl opposite, the player takes the stones and places them in their own Mancala. The player also gets another turn.
8. Each player moves across the board depositing stones in each of the bowls. The aim of the game is to deposit as many stones as possible in your own Mancala and the player with the most stones win.

➕ Health & Safety

Closely supervise the activity to ensure younger children do not put the stones in their mouth.

What you need:

- Parents, carers and extended families
- A space for families to get together and chat
- A parent newsletter or an invitation to a parents and carers meeting or forum

Top tip

Invite a more experienced parent or carer to the meeting to champion the parent buddy scheme.

What's in it for the children?

This activity is about making a welcoming and inclusive culture and recognising the unique parenting journeys made by families at the setting. Pairing new and experienced parents and carers can strengthen their confidence, which in turn benefits their children.

Taking it forward

- Create a parent and carer notice board in your setting, to display the dates of the meetings and give details of the parent buddy scheme. This is a positive way to show how the scheme is part of the regular activities in the setting.

✚ Health & Safety

Provide guidelines to ensure that all parents and carers are aware of the setting's professional and safeguarding boundaries.

What to do:

1. Invite current parents and carers to a meeting to discuss the idea of a parent buddy scheme.
2. At the meeting, explain the purpose of such a scheme: to support parents and carers whose children will be joining the setting. For some parents and carers, starting nursery is a scary process, but also creates an opportunity where they can start to make friends.
3. Discuss the possibility of using the scheme for swapping resources and equipment, such as buggies, or attending training or workshops together, such as first-aid courses.
4. Agree a plan for how to connect new parents and carers with more experienced parents and carers, and discuss confidentiality and safeguarding.
5. Once the plan is in place, ask new parents and carers if they are happy to have a parent buddy when their child is settling into the nursery.
6. Build in a feedback system so that you can know whether the buddy scheme is successful.
7. Organise a parents and carers coffee morning to share the findings.

Dorothy's tea party

Sharing the children's world

What you need:

- A special bear
- A tea set
- A teapot
- Tea and coffee for adults
- Tea for children (mint is ideal)
- A selection of party tea food, such as cakes and sandwiches

What to do:

1. Explain to the children that special visitors will be joining them for tea with Dorothy the bear.
2. Explain that because they will be expecting guests they need to get everything ready.
3. Ask the children to wash their hands.
4. Help the children to set out the tea and the food that has been prepared.
5. Supervise the children in making tea for the bear.
6. Encourage the children to welcome their parents and carers when they arrive and to offer them tea or coffee (to be served by an adult).

Top tip ⭐

Prepare the sandwiches and cakes with the children earlier in the day to provide an opportunity for multi-layered learning.

What's in it for the children?

The children are able to share their world with their families in an unhurried moment, whilst beginning to learn the art of conversation.

Taking it forward

- The setting's bear can be invited home to meet the children's family for tea, thereby building a bridge into the children's homes.

 Health & Safety

A risk assessment for preparing hot drinks should be carried out and any potential allergies identified.

Finding my place in the neighbourhood
Building a sense of belonging

What you need:

- A map of the local area
- Some knowledge of the local area

Top tip

Make a photo album of the trips to keep in the children's book corner for them to enjoy.

What's in it for the children?

This activity is often framed as a multi-generational approach. It helps develop inclusive practice and supports children and staff to take their place among their local communities. Nurseries are community catalysts and need to recognise the power they have to create local networks and to make connections with people of all ages, backgrounds and experiences. Going out into the neighbourhood also builds a sense of belonging by making the environment familiar and provides an opportunity for the children to meet a diverse range of people.

Taking it forward

- Plan regular trips and outings and build them into your weekly plans.
- Make links with a care home where the children can send regular letters and artwork.

Health & Safety

Carry out risk assessments of all trips and outings.

What to do:

Take the children out into the local community to learn new and exciting things. Possible activities include:

1. Meet the local 'Big Issue' seller, ask them their name, say hello and buy a magazine.
2. Buy fruit from the local fruit seller.
3. Identify the bus and train stations so that the children learn markers in their community.
4. Find the local parks and green spaces to explore.
5. Build networks with the local community to ensure these links become regular and frequent and children begin to feel a sense of belonging with where they live. For example, elderly care homes, children's centres, dentists, libraries, museums, art galleries, theatres; invite people to visit the nursery to meet the children.

Food bank

Thinking of others

What you need:

- Food donations
- Boxes to collect and store the donations
- Transport to take the donations to another setting

Top tip ⭐

Encourage the children to think about this activity not as one between a giver and receiver, but as a gesture of friendship.

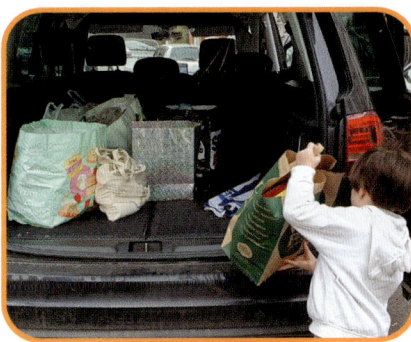

What's In It for the children?

The children will learn to think of others, show empathy and to develop a 'can-do' approach to solving problems within our society.

Taking it forward

- Support the children in writing to their local supermarkets for more donations.

➕ Health & Safety

Check the expiry dates and the packaging of all the food that has been donated.

What to do:

1. Make links with community settings that can benefit from this project.
2. During circle time introduce the children to food and why we need to eat.
3. Ask the children what they buy when they go shopping.
4. Invite the children to list their favourite foods at nursery and at home.
5. Talk to the children about food banks and why they exist.
6. Support the children to write letters to their families asking for food donations.

Web of connectivity

Strengthening relationships between staff

What you need:

- A ball of wool
- Scissors

Top tip

Connection without judgement builds trust and energy that sustains relationships.

What's in it for the children?

Children benefit from attending a setting where staff have strong and harmonious relationships. By sharing connections, a more inclusive environment is created.

Taking it forward

- Repeat this activity when a new member of staff joins the setting.

✚ Health & Safety

Ensure all colleagues are aware of the need for confidentiality and are clear about how the information will be used.

What to do:

1. Explain the purpose of the activity to your colleagues, which is to strengthen connections by sharing some personal information.

2. Remind colleagues you are accessing a part of their private lives so confidentiality is extremely important.

3. Form a circle, standing or sitting. You decide!

4. Ask one person to hold the ball of wool and start by sharing something about themselves or something they like to do.

5. If this information provides a connection with someone else in the room, ask that person to call out. For example, if someone says 'I went to school in Stratford' someone else might say, 'My Grandma lived in Stratford'.

6. The person holding the ball of wool throws it to the person who has called out, whilst holding onto the start of the wool.

7. Continue sharing personal information and passing the ball of wool between each other until a web has formed.

8. When everyone has held the ball of wool at least once, use a pair of sharp scissors to cut the connecting strings, symbolising that we must all return to our own lives, but that we all remain part of the group and must keep working together to remain connected.

9. Each person should end up with some wool, which they can tie around their wrist as a reminder of their connections with their colleagues.

Take my hand
Coaching conversations

What you need:

- Staff who are able to lead coaching conversations to support staff pedagogically

Top tip

Think of every conversation as a coaching conversation.

What to do:

Coaching is a powerful way to encourage and support staff to develop, deepen and apply their skills and knowledge with greater competence and assurance.

1. Coaching conversations are designed to help staff reflect on a particular issue by framing questions to help them understand better and usually develop the action needed through the conversation.

2. Coaching is thinking out loud with the help of an empathetic and trustworthy colleague.

3. Frame the coaching around questions such as:
   - What do you want to achieve from this coaching session?
   - What would you like to happen with…?
   - What result are you trying to achieve?
   - What do you want to change?
   - What would the benefits be if you achieved this goal?
   - What outcome would be ideal?

What's in it for the children?

Many staff are unsure about diversity and inclusion and shy away from it, but developing a coaching approach across the setting will lead to an increase in confidence and improved pedagogical competence. Coaching builds empathy, sensitivity and develops better listening, all of which will benefit the children.

Taking it forward

- Consider enrolling staff on a coaching programme or using a coaching model as part of your practice.

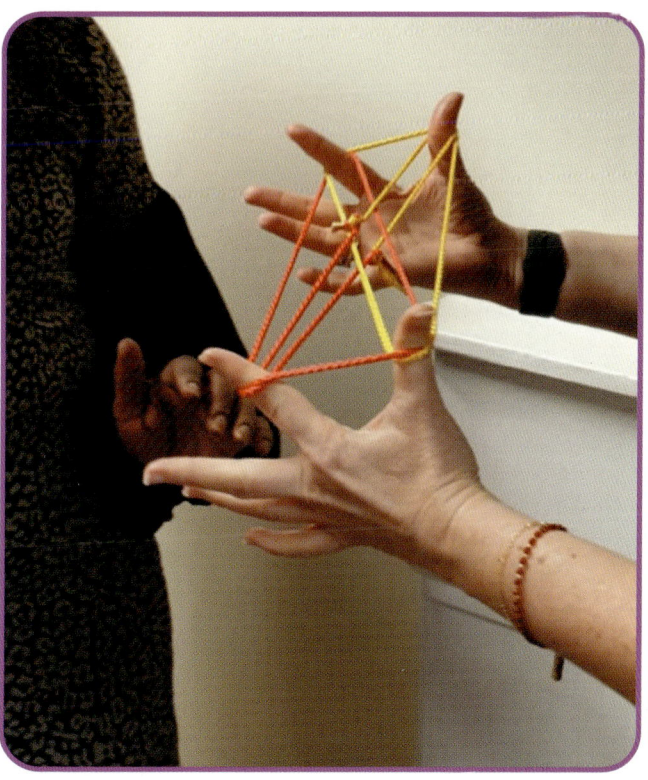

Build a social inclusion network

Developing a culture of inclusion

What you need:

- Contact details for colleagues from those settings interested in the network
- A clear idea of what the aims of your social inclusion network will be
- Understanding of how to build a network
- Time and space to meet or a virtual meeting platform if meeting online

Top tip

Think about how you might use social media to share the network stories.

What's in it for the children?

Children benefit from having better informed teachers who are able to develop a culture of inclusion.

Taking it forward

- Open out the network to a wider group of colleagues in different settings, such as local childminders, pre-schools and after-school settings.

✚ Health & Safety

Be aware of data protection laws and pay attention to the rules of GDPR in relevant situations, for example if you are recording the sessions or using case studies.

What to do:

Building a network of practitioners to share and extend learning will be most successful if it is shaped by an inclusive approach and framed by the values of a community of practice. The following questions should be considered:

- What will I bring to the network?
- What will I gain from being part of the network?
- How can I test and implement the learning in my setting?
- How can I help tell the network story?

1. Contact a group of colleagues and suggest that you meet once a month either on screen or in person. Use the questions above to help the network to shape its terms of reference.

2. Plan a simple agenda to give shape to the meeting. Agree who will chair and take notes.

3. Invite colleagues to add their comments and suggestions prior to the meeting.

4. Open each session with a question, a challenge or a new piece of research or alternate each meeting with a guest speaker. At the following meeting talk about how the new information was used in the settings.